**BE A
BETTER**
Real Estate
AGENT

REAL ESTATE LISTINGS LIKE A PRO

Your Guide to Winning and Wowing Sellers

**Mini
Mastery**
Series

Donna Wysinger

Dedication

To the listing legends, mentors, and colleagues who have taught me that representing a seller is both an honor and an art ...

Thank you for sharing your strategies, stories, and support. Your influence has shaped how I prepare, present, and protect my clients' best interests, and I carry those lessons into every listing I take.

To my amazing clients, friends, and family ...

Your trust, loyalty, and referrals have been the key to my success. Every home I've listed, every challenge we've overcome together, and every joyful closing day has been possible because of you.

This book is for you, and for the countless sellers whose stories are yet to be written.

Thank you.

TABLE OF CONTENTS

TABLE OF CONTENTS

- Your Head Start to a Smooth Sale Guide
- Preparing Your Home for Success Checklist
- Your Personal "Signature Service" Toolkit
- Weekly Market Update Sample
- Surprise and Delight at Your Open House
- Closing Week Countdown
- Self-Care for Success: Little Rituals for Big Impact

Foreword

Listings are the heartbeat of a thriving real estate business. They give you the leverage, visibility, and credibility to grow faster, serve more deeply, and build a career you truly love.

But landing a listing and guiding it from "For Sale" to "Sold" is so much more than a checklist of tasks. It's about understanding your seller's needs, crafting a plan that inspires confidence, and showing up as the steady, skilled professional they can trust through every twist and turn.

This book was designed to walk you through the entire listing journey, from that very first "Hello" to the follow up long after closing, with practical steps, creative ideas, and systems you can make your own. Whether you're brand new to the business or a seasoned agent looking to refine your process, you'll find strategies here to help you stand out, serve with excellence, and keep your pipeline full.

It's my hope that you'll use these pages as both a guide and a source of inspiration — something you can come back to whenever you need fresh ideas, renewed motivation, or a reminder that you have everything it takes to be a powerhouse listing agent.

Now, let's dive in and turn your listings into lasting success stories.

Donna Wysinger
Owner/Founder
Be a Better Agent

Why LISTINGS Matter
(and Why Sellers Need You)

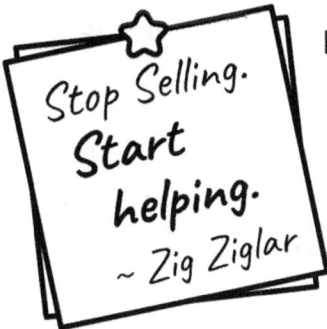

Stop Selling.
Start helping.
~ Zig Ziglar

If you're holding this book in your hands, you're likely someone who wants to get better, not just at business, but at building real, lasting relationships in real estate.

... Or, your Broker gave you this book because they want you to succeed.

... OR, a friend gifted you this book because you said one too many times that you wanted a successful real estate business, and you weren't sure exactly what to do.

So, here is the first secret: You want to lead with service, grow with confidence, and create a business that not only thrives, but feels good to run. That's why this book was written, and why *listings* matter more than ever.

When I first started in real estate soooo many years ago, I didn't start with the confidence needed to find, acquire, and *win* listings. All I could think about was that a home was most people's largest asset and it wasn't something I felt brave enough to handle.

I was much more comfortable working with homebuyers. We all held the belief that buyers weren't "paying" for our services and just needed help seeing homes and negotiating the deals. I could do this!

I would hear comments among my colleagues like, "List to last..." and I honestly had very little idea about what they really meant. Surely I could build a career just helping buyers, right?

Fortunately, I eventually realized something that changed everything: working with sellers gave me the structure, the flow, and the predictability that allowed me to grow in a way that aligned with my values.

Don't get me wrong. Buyers are a delight, and those relationships are meaningful. I have always enjoyed working with buyers, especially first-time homebuyers because it feels so good helping them realize their home ownership goals.

However, it was **mastering listings** that gave me leverage, confidence, and space to serve more people at a higher level. And not just once... but over and over again.

What made that possible? **Successful Systems. Stellar Strategies. Superb Service.** And of course, a whole lot of heart.

As part of my real estate journey, I also spent time working on mega teams as an assistant, as a transaction coordinator, and as a marketing designer and manager.

So, it's not just my own experience of being in the trenches with listings, presentations, negotiations, and closings that has given me the experience I am now sharing with you.

As a part of larger teams, working with lots of listings and home sellers, and making a lot more money... I began to see something that many agents miss: **the magic is in the repeatable**. It's in the conversations you master. The systems, checklists, and materials you create. The way you educate your sellers. The tools you provide. The way you *follow up* and *follow all the way through* the transaction. And the way you stay connected long after the sign comes down.

This guide will **walk you through the entire journey,** from the time a seller raises their hand, to the moment you deliver the keys *(and beyond)*. Each chapter is designed to give you simple, repeatable tools and strategies that build trust, demonstrate value, and deepen client loyalty.

You will learn how to:

- **Follow up with seller leads** using meaningful emails, texts, and items of value

- **Create an unforgettable listing presentation** (that doesn't feel salesy)

- **Set up homes for maximum market impact**, with systems that take the pressure off

- **Communicate with clarity** throughout showings, offers, inspections, and contracts

- **Support sellers during every phase,** including after the sale

- Build a **signature seller system** that reflects your strengths and builds your brand

Sellers need you. Not just someone who puts a sign in the yard and hopes for the best, but a true professional. A steady guide. A trusted resource. Someone who makes the process smoother, less stressful, and even a little fun.

Whether you're a brand-new agent learning how to talk to your first seller or a seasoned professional ready to refine your systems, this book was written for you.

Let's build something amazing and wildly effective together.

CHAPTER 1

HELLO SELLER!
Lead Capture & First Impressions

There is a critical moment in every listing journey: the *first impression*. Whether a seller reaches out directly or you're referred by someone in your sphere, how you capture that moment and what happens next sets the tone for everything that follows.

This chapter is about what happens *before* the listing presentation. Because long before you ever walk through the front door with a clipboard in hand, you have a chance to do something powerful:

- Build trust.
- Demonstrate value.
- Start the relationship on the right foot.

Real success is built on real connection.

And it all begins with how you follow up.

✋ Lead Capture: Be Ready When They Raise Their Hand

In today's world, seller leads can come from anywhere; online ads, social media, postcards, networking events, or good old-fashioned referrals. The moment someone expresses even the slightest interest in selling, it's important to treat that lead like gold.

But here's the key: **respond quickly, warmly, and with purpose**. Sellers are often nervous, uncertain, or over-whelmed, and they're watching how you handle the small things to decide if they trust you with the BIG thing (their home!).

Have a system in place for:

- Prompt replies (within an hour if possible)
- A pre-written but personalized response for first contact
- Capturing their name, contact info, and how they found you
- A place to store your notes and track follow-up *(CRM, spreadsheet, or even a simple folder system)*

Warm, Helpful Emails and Texts: Connection Before Conversion

Let's face it, most real estate emails sound the same: generic, salesy, and forgettable. That's not you.

Instead, use the first follow up to reflect who you are: a helpful, kind, confident guide who genuinely wants to serve.

Here's a sample email you can tailor:

Subject: Great Connecting with You – Let's Explore Your Home's Next Chapter

Hi [Seller's Name],

It was so nice to hear that you're starting to think about selling your home. That's a big decision, and my goal is to make the process as smooth, clear, and successful as possible for you.

When the time feels right, I'd love to set up a quick visit to walk through your home and chat about your goals, timeline, and any questions you have. I've also attached a simple resource to help you begin thinking about your next steps.

No pressure. I'm just here to help.

Warmly,

[Your Name]

Follow up with a friendly text message that says:

"Hi [Name], just sent over an email with some helpful info whenever you're ready. No rush at all. I'm just happy to help whenever you need!"

PRO TIP

It's all about showing you're responsive, but not pushy. That balance helps build trust.

Branded Items of Value: Be Helpful, Not Salesy 🏅

Once that first contact is made, use **items of value** to stay on their radar. These small, branded touches add professionalism and personality without screaming *"sales pitch."*

Ideas to consider:

- **"Thinking of Selling?" checklist** – branded with your info, mailed or emailed
- **Market snapshot flyer** – showing activity in their neighborhood
- **Seller Success Stories** – a short PDF with testimonials from past sellers
- **"Get Seller Ready" PDF or postcard** – with staging tips, timing tips, or a home maintenance checklist

These pieces aren't about convincing them to sell, they're about **positioning you as the guide they can trust** when the time comes.

And remember: make your items of value beautiful. Use your branding colors, fonts, and logo. Consistency builds credibility.

> **PRO TIP** Have folders already prepared with your checklists, FAQs, sample postcards, etc. and then simply add the market snapshot or CMA to the folder before the listing appointment.

Building Trust Before the Appointment 🛡️

If a seller schedules a listing appointment with you, you're already halfway there. But don't stop nurturing that trust just yet.

Between the "yes" and the actual appointment:

- Send a friendly confirmation text or email with what to expect
- Include a seller prep guide or FAQ sheet so they feel informed
- Reiterate that your goal is to understand their needs, not pressure them to list

When you show up, you're not a stranger. You've already been a helpful, trustworthy resource. That's powerful.

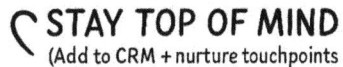

⚙️ Your System in Action

CONTACT RECEIVED
(Call, text, referral, online form)

↓

SEND WARM EMAIL + TEXT
(Include item of value)

↓

DELIVER HELPFUL RESOURCE
(Checklist, market report, etc.)

↓

SCHEDULE LISTING APPOINTMENT
(Confirm and prep seller)

↓

STAY TOP OF MIND
(Add to CRM + nurture touchpoints)

To make this flow easily in your business, I recommend having a simple **Seller Lead Welcome Kit** that includes:

- Email and text templates
- 3-5 branded PDFs or printables
- Notes on their property and timeline
- A CRM or follow-up log (checklist)

This allows you to stay consistent while keeping things warm and personalized. No more reinventing the wheel every time someone says, "We're thinking of selling..."

First Impressions Matter - and Follow Through Is KEY

This chapter is where that magic begins.

You don't have to be perfect, but people remember how you made them feel. When a seller reaches out, they're hoping for clarity. **They want to feel safe, supported, and seen.**

And, when you **combine a responsive system with your authentic care**, you turn casual inquiries into confident clients and set the stage for everything that follows.

Let's move into the next chapter where you'll learn to shine even brighter during *the listing appointment.*

🔑 Key Reflections

How do I want a potential seller to feel after their first interaction with me?

_____

_____

_____

_____

_____

What email or text template can I create today that would save me time and build trust in future follow-ups?

_____

_____

_____

_____

_____

What branded item of value could I design or update this week that would truly help a seller?

_____

_____

_____

_____

_____

_____

NOTES

CHAPTER 2

The LISTING Appointment
Shine and SERVE

The listing appointment is your moment to show up, connect, and prove that you're the agent who will not just list their home, but guide them through one of the biggest transactions of their life with skill, care, and professionalism.

When you listen deeply, sellers hear confidence — not a pitch.

This isn't about dazzling with hype or dominating the conversation. It's about combining preparation, presence, and genuine curiosity to create a meeting that leaves the seller thinking:

> *"I trust them. I feel safe with them.*
> *I want to work with them."*

Let's walk through how to make that happen.

📑 Preparing a Winning Listing Presentation

The best listing appointments begin *long before* you step through the front door.

Preparation shows respect ... for their time, for their home, and for the decision they're about to make. Your goal is to arrive not just with information, but with insights tailored to their property, their neighborhood, and their goals.

Your Pre-Appointment Prep Checklist:

- **Research their property**: square footage, year built, tax records, last sale price, any building permits.
- **Pull comparables**: recent sales, active listings, and expired listings in the neighborhood.
- **Prepare a custom Comparable Market Analysis (CMA).** Focus on market activity that's relevant to their property's size, location, and features.
- **Know the neighborhood**: schools, parks, amenities, upcoming developments.
- **Print or load your visuals**: a polished, branded listing packet or presentation (digital or printed) that includes:
  - Your marketing plan
  - Your pricing strategy
  - Examples of your photography, staging, and property descriptions
  - Testimonials and success stories from past sellers

Creating a Calm, Confident In-Person Experience

When you arrive at the appointment, remember: the seller is evaluating you from the moment they open the door, not just for competence, but for comfort. Your tone, body language, and energy matter as much as your expertise. Sellers need to feel both at ease and confident in your ability.

Best Practices for a Calm, Confident Consultation:

- Arrive a few minutes early *(but not too early).*
- Dress professionally, in line with your brand.
- Carry your materials neatly. Avoid juggling papers or fumbling with tech.
- Start with genuine conversation before launching into business.
- Tour the home together, listening to their stories and noting features they love.

Think of this as a two-way interview. You're there to earn their trust and to decide if you're the right fit for each other.

How to Listen Deeply and Identify the Seller's Goals 🎯

One of the fastest ways to stand out is simple: listen more than you talk. Many agents race to "prove" themselves by rattling off facts, stats, and marketing plans. But sellers want to feel heard before they want to be impressed. Ask open-ended questions like:

- "What matters most to you in this sale?"
- "What is your ideal timeline?"
- "Have you sold a home before? What was that experience like?"
- "Are there any worries or challenges you're anticipating?"

As they answer, take notes (either on paper or tablet) so they know you value their input. These details become the foundation for your recommendations and your follow-up.

Follow-Up That Continues the Conversation and Shows True Value

Even if you think you nailed the appointment, the follow-up is where many agents lose the listing. Sellers often meet with more than one agent and the one who stays connected thoughtfully is often the one they choose.

Your Post-Appointment Follow-Up System:

- **Same Day** – Send a thank-you email or text expressing appreciation for their time and reiterating one key point you discussed.

- **Within 24–48 Hours** – Deliver any promised materials (updated comps, staging recommendations, pricing scenarios).
- **Ongoing** – If they're not ready to sign yet, keep them on your "active nurture" list with relevant items of value, not generic "Just checking in" messages.

Example Follow-Up Text or Email Verbiage:

"Hi [Name], thank you again for welcoming me into your home yesterday. I loved hearing about how you've cared for the garden all these years. It's such a beautiful feature that I know buyers will notice. I'm attaching the updated market analysis we discussed, and a few staging suggestions tailored to your property. Please don't hesitate to reach out with any questions. I'm here to help in any way you need."

This keeps you in their mind as the helpful, prepared, and professional choice.

Be Their Confident Guide

The listing appointment isn't just about convincing someone to hire you, it's about **building a relationship based on trust, understanding, and value**. When you prepare thoroughly, create a calm and confident space, listen deeply, and follow up with care, you set yourself apart in a sea of agents.

🔑 Key Reflections

How can I improve my pre-appointment preparation so it feels more personal for each seller?

_____

_____

_____

_____

_____

What questions could I add to my appointment that would help uncover a seller's deeper motivations?

_____

_____

_____

_____

_____

How can I make my follow-up more valuable than a simple "check-in"?

_____

_____

_____

_____

_____

_____

NOTES

DOODLES

CHAPTER **3**

Ready... Set... ACTION!
Preparing the Property to Sell

Winning effort begins with Preparation!

The way a property looks, feels, and presents itself to the market can determine how fast it sells, and for how much. A home that shines not only attracts more buyers but often sparks stronger offers and smoother negotiations.

In this chapter, we'll walk through how to guide sellers from "lived in" to "market ready" without overwhelming them, while using smart systems and your expertise to make the process as stress-free as possible.

Home Prep Walkthroughs and Timelines

Before any photos are taken or buyers walk through the door, the home needs to be evaluated with a buyer's eye, and that's where your pre-listing walkthrough comes in.

Your Home Prep Walkthrough Process:

- **Schedule early** — ideally as soon as the seller commits to working with you (or sooner if they're still deciding).
- **Walk the property with fresh eyes** — both inside and outside.
- **Point out quick wins first** — lightbulb changes, deep cleaning, decluttering.
- **Address high-impact upgrades** — fresh paint, minor repairs, updated hardware.
- **Prioritize based on timeline and budget** — not every improvement is worth the investment for every property.

Timelines matter. Create a prep schedule with milestones so the seller knows what's happening and when. A visual checklist helps keep them on track and reduces last-minute stress.

> **PRO TIP** Give them a branded "Prepping for Market" checklist they can physically check off. It makes progress visible and keeps the momentum going.

Photos, Tours, and Virtual Marketing 📷

Once the home is prepped, it's time to capture it at its best. Professional photography is non-negotiable. A buyer's first impression almost always happens online, and poor visuals can turn away even the most interested prospects.

Your Marketing Media Toolkit:

- **Professional Photos** — capture the best angles, natural light, and inviting spaces.
- **3D Tours / Virtual Walkthroughs** — especially valuable for out-of-town buyers.
- **Drone Photography** — highlights lot size, location, and unique features.
- **Lifestyle Shots** — show the home as part of a living experience *(nearby parks, community spaces, neighborhood charm)*.

PRO TIP Always attend your photo session or coordinate with your photographer to ensure the property is staged exactly as you want it: pillows fluffed, lights on, blinds positioned perfectly.

⌂ Staging Tips

Staging is not about making a home look like a magazine, it's about helping buyers imagine living there. This means creating a clean, neutral, and welcoming environment where buyers can picture their own lives unfolding. The right staging draws attention to the home's best features, minimizes distractions, and helps every room tell a story that invites buyers to stay a little longer... and fall in love.

Staging Essentials:

- Declutter rooms to showcase space
- Use neutral colors with a few warm accents
- Arrange furniture to highlight flow and focal points
- Add fresh flowers or plants for life and freshness
- Remove personal photos and overly unique décor

Repairs and Remodeling 🛠️

For some homes, the prep may involve more than quick touch-ups. Many homeowners have deferred some maintenance and updating, and they may feel like the property can only be sold "as is" *(or not at all)*. Show those sellers the numbers for selling their property without remodeling or repairs and how much more they will gain by addressing issues ahead of time.

You can help your sellers by recommending changes and suggesting some of your preferred vendors to make them. They will appreciate your guidance and expertise.

Concierge Services are another option which could be a benefit for sellers that don't feel they have the money to pay for costly upgrading and updating. A concierge service can evaluate your client's home and determine what they can do to make the property "Market Ready" and how much it will cost. They coordinate repairs, updates, and even staging, and these services can be paid for from the seller proceeds.

This approach removes stress for the seller and ensures the home goes to market in its best condition without upfront costs.

🌹 The Psychology of Presentation and First Impressions

Buyers form opinions within seconds of seeing a home, whether that's pulling into the driveway or scrolling through the first listing photo. Your job is to control that moment.

Curb Appeal Matters:

- Mow the lawn, trim bushes, and weed flower beds.
- Power wash siding, decks, and driveways.
- Add a pop of color with a door wreath or potted plants.

Inside the Home:

- Ensure it smells fresh. Avoid heavy air fresheners.
- Let in natural light. Open blinds and curtains.
- Set a comfortable temperature.

When buyers feel "at home," they're more likely to explore with excitement rather than hesitation.

Set the Stage, Start Strong 📢

Prepping a home for the market is about more than cleaning and decluttering, it's about creating an emotional connection and making sure every detail supports the asking price. When you walk sellers through a clear, achievable plan and combine it with professional marketing, you set the property *(and your relationship with the seller)* up for success.

🔑 Key Reflections

What consistent systems do I have in place to prepare
every listing for maximum buyer appeal?

_____

_____

_____

_____

_____

How can I adapt my staging and marketing approach to
suit different sellers, price points, and property styles?

_____

_____

_____

_____

_____

In what ways can I make the preparation process a
positive, confidence-building experience for every seller
I work with?

_____

_____

_____

_____

_____

NOTES

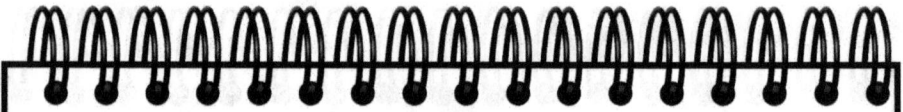

DOODLES

CHAPTER 4

Launch with LOVE
Listing the Property

The *"go live"* moment is one of the most exciting stages in the seller's journey. It's the day their home steps onto the stage and introduces itself to the world, and your job is to make that debut unforgettable.

> A great launch turns a listing into a must see.

A listing launch isn't just about uploading details to the MLS and hoping buyers show up. It's a strategic, coordinated effort that blends storytelling, smart marketing, and purposeful networking.

When you launch with intention *(and yes, a little love)*, you give your seller's home the best chance to shine and capture the attention it deserves.

Writing Irresistible Property Descriptions ✏️

The first thing most buyers see after the photos is the description, and in just a few sentences, it can either spark curiosity or get lost in the scroll.

Keys to an Irresistible Description:

- **Lead with a hook** – something unique about the home, location, or lifestyle.
- **Paint a picture** – use descriptive language that helps buyers feel the space.
- **Highlight benefits, not just features** – *"Spacious backyard perfect for summer barbecues,"* instead of *"Large backyard."*
- **Keep it concise** – avoid filler words and make it easy to skim.

💡 **PRO TIP** Write for people, not just algorithms. While keywords help for searchability, a well-told story sells the home.

Example:

"Welcome to your peaceful retreat in the heart of Willow Creek! This light-filled, single-level home offers an open floor plan perfect for gatherings, a chef's kitchen with granite counters, and a backyard oasis with room to garden, play, and relax under the stars."

🏠 MLS Optimization

Your MLS listing is the hub from which most other marketing pulls its data. So, it's worth getting every detail right.

MLS Must-Dos:

- **Use all available photo slots** — buyers are more likely to click on a listing with multiple high-quality images.
- **Double-check accuracy** — square footage, lot size, number of rooms, and amenities should be correct.
- **Fill in all fields** — the more complete the listing, the better it ranks in searches.
- Place key selling points in the **first two lines** of the description (often what's shown in preview mode).
- Use **clear, searchable keywords** for location, style, and features.
- Preview the MLS listing before going live to make sure it formats correctly on different devices.

📄 Using Social Media, Email Marketing, and Flyers Effectively

A strong launch strategy goes beyond the MLS. The more ways you share the listing, the faster you build interest and momentum.

Social Media:

- Share a *"Just Listed"* post with your best 1–3 photos and a clear call-to-action.

- Use Stories or Reels to give a behind-the-scenes peek at the home.
- Tag the location and use relevant hashtags to reach local buyers and agents.

Email Marketing:

- Send a dedicated "New Listing" email to your database with photos, property details, and open house info.
- Segment your list so the right people see the right properties.

Flyers and Print Materials:

- Create visually appealing flyers for open houses, community boards, and to leave inside the home.
- Include a QR code linking to the full online listing or virtual tour.

Announcing the Listing to Your Sphere and Agent Network

Your sphere of influence and professional network can be some of your strongest launch partners.

Sphere:

- Call or text past clients who might know someone looking in that area.
- Share a personalized note in your monthly newsletter.

Agent Network:

- Email the listing to agents who've recently sold in the neighborhood or work with buyers in that price range.
- Post in local agent Facebook groups or MLS forums.
- Position your announcement as an opportunity, not just information. For example: *"Just listed a three bedroom in Maplewood with the backyard everyone wants — would love to see if you have buyers before it's gone!"*

🚀 Launch Like It Matters *(Because It Does)*

The launch is more than a step on the checklist, it's the moment your seller's home takes center stage. When you combine compelling storytelling, optimized MLS details, targeted marketing, and intentional networking, you create the kind of buzz that drives showings, offers, and excitement.

And remember... a successful launch not only helps the sale — it sets the tone for the repeat business and referrals that come from doing things right.

🔑 Key Reflections

How can I make each property's launch feel unique and special to the seller?

_____

_____

_____

_____

_____

How can I adapt my staging and marketing approach to suit different sellers, price points, and property styles?

_____

_____

_____

_____

How can I track which marketing channels give my listings the most engagement?

_____

_____

_____

_____

_____

_____

NOTES

DOODLES

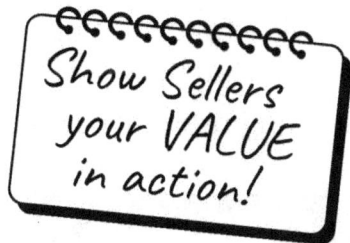

CHAPTER 5

Stay CONNECTED
Communication Builds Confidence

When a listing hits the market, excitement runs high. The photos and virtual tours are beautiful, the listing is live, and anticipation fills the air. But once the "For Sale" sign is planted, your job is far from over. In fact, this is when the real relationship-building begins. Sellers want to feel informed, guided, and supported every step of the way, and that's exactly where you shine.

> Show Sellers your VALUE in action!

You want to keep your sellers confident, comfortable, and ready for action. From showing prep to follow-up communication, your ability to educate and encourage will make the difference between an anxious seller and a relaxed, trusting client who happily refers you for years to come.

37

🏠 Showing Appointments Protocol

During the active listing phase, your Sellers want to know all about their showings! Are they happening? How many are we getting? What are buyers saying?

Post-showing follow-up is one of the most valuable and often overlooked services you can provide. The key is to share useful, constructive feedback without creating panic or frustration.

First, make sure you have a good follow-up plan between yourself and the agents who are showing your listing to buyers. Do your best to glean feedback from every agent that walks through a property so you can share this information with your sellers. Most showing services provide follow up emails and/or texts to agents requesting feedback. Be sure your app settings are sending requests at least 3 times after a showing.

> **PRO TIP**
>
> Send your own additional feedback requests by text. Be sure to include a photo and enough info about the house that the agent knows exactly which listing you are asking about. When they respond, be sure to send a thank you.

Keep your seller informed throughout every request for a showing; when you receive the request, the time the showing will happen, whether the showing *did* actually occur, and then any feedback you receive.

Sample follow-up email or text template:

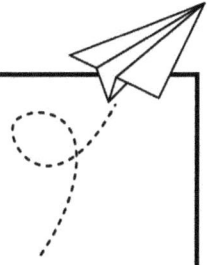

> **Subject**: Showing Feedback for
> [Property Address]
>
> Hi [Seller Name],
>
> We had a showing today. Here's the feedback they provided:
>
> **Positive Notes**: [List compliments from buyers.]
>
> **Opportunities**: [Gently share areas they felt could improve.]
>
> This feedback is valuable because it gives us insight into how buyers are perceiving the home. I'll keep tracking trends and share recommendations if we see consistent patterns.
>
> You're doing a great job keeping the home showing ready. Thank you!

This approach keeps sellers informed while positioning you as their calm, capable guide.

Weekly Market Updates 🏠

One of the best ways to keep sellers confident is to stay in regular contact and keep them informed. The last thing you want to be is the agent that sellers complain about, *"All they did was stick a sign in my yard and put my house on the MLS. And then they disappeared!"*

Weekly market updates will help give your sellers relevant information *and* peace of mind. These short, easy-to-read reports should include:

- Number of showings in the past week
- Feedback received from buyer agents
- New competing listings that have come on the market
- Recent sales in the area *(and their sale prices)*
- Any notable market shifts or buyer trends

Even if there's little activity, your updates show the seller you're actively monitoring their listing and staying engaged. This reassurance is often the difference between a seller feeling "ignored" and feeling like they're your top priority.

📋 Showing Tips and Guides for Sellers

When sending your Weekly Market Update, include a meaningful item of value, something that offers your sellers practical, insightful guidance for presenting their home at its very best. This small but intentional addition reinforces your commitment to their success and helps them feel supported every step of the way.

Ideas for items of value to include:

- 20 Staging Tips to Help You Sell
- 12 Great Tips for Showing Your Home
- Improve Your Home's Curb Appeal
- Seasonal Home Maintenance Tips
- Best and Worst Last-Minute Hiding Places

Emotional Support and Mindset Encouragement 🤝
During Quiet Times

Every agent knows there are lulls. Weeks with only a few showings can be discouraging for sellers, especially in a slower market. This is when your role as **confidence coach** is most important.

- Acknowledge the slow patch, don't ignore it.
- Remind them of market realities and seasonal patterns.
- Reaffirm your plan and any steps you're taking to generate fresh interest.
- Offer encouragement with small, personal touches; a quick phone call, a handwritten note, or even a lighthearted text that shows you're thinking of them.

When sellers feel heard and supported during slow times, they're far more likely to stay patient and trust the process.

💡 Help Your Sellers "See the Light"

When a property has been on the market for several weeks with only a handful of showings, it may be a sign that the price is higher than the market will bear in your area. On the other hand, if you've had steady showings (thanks to your excellent marketing) but no offers, it often points to a condition concern, something buyers can't fully assess until they step inside.

This is where your role as a *trusted guide* comes in. By thoughtfully reviewing feedback from buyer's agents, you can help sellers identify any recurring themes, whether it's a bold paint color, worn flooring, or needed repairs. Sometimes, these condition concerns can be addressed directly; other times, a strategic price adjustment is the clearest solution.

The beauty of consistently sending **Weekly Market Updates** and including helpful resources like *"Pricing Your Home Right,"* is that you empower your sellers to come to their own realizations. When you provide relevant information and insights week after week, sellers often approach *you* first, asking whether it's time to refresh those walls, replace that carpet, or make a price change to attract stronger interest. You've built a foundation of trust, so even sensitive conversations feel collaborative, not confrontational.

Support That Sells

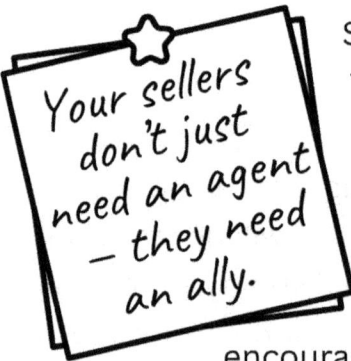

Your sellers don't just need an agent — they need an ally.

Showing support isn't just about the showings themselves — it's about showing up for your clients in ways that matter most to them. By providing practical checklists, clear updates, thoughtful follow-ups, and steady encouragement, you help sellers feel confident and cared for from listing day to closing day.

🔑 Key Reflections

How consistent is my showing prep guidance across all my listings?

_____

_____

_____

_____

_____

Do my weekly updates answer the questions sellers have before they even ask?

_____

_____

_____

_____

_____

How can I bring more personal encouragement to sellers during slower weeks?

_____

_____

_____

_____

_____

NOTES

CHAPTER 6

Open House MAGIC
Showcase with STYLE

An OPEN HOUSE is more than a tour — it's an invitation to DREAM.

Open houses are more than just a real estate tradition, they're an opportunity to shine, to connect, and to showcase a home in its very best light.

Done well, an open house can attract serious buyers, spark buzz in the community, and reassure your sellers *(and their friends and neighbors)* that you are going above and beyond to get their property noticed.

This chapter will guide you through planning, hosting, and following up so every open house leaves a lasting impression.

Planning and Promoting Open Houses 🏠

The magic begins well before the first guest walks through the door. Start by collaborating with your sellers to choose the right date and time — aiming for when your target buyers are most likely to be out and about.

Once the date is set, create a layered marketing plan:

- **MLS Posting**: Add the open house details and be sure the home's photos and description are irresistible.
- **Social Media**: Post on your business and personal pages, neighborhood groups, and Instagram Stories. A quick "sneak peek" video from the home can spark interest.
- **Email Invitations**: Send an e-blast to your sphere and fellow agents, inviting them to share with their own networks.
- **Signage**: Use clear, branded signs placed strategically throughout the neighborhood. Add balloons or flags to draw attention.
- **Neighborhood Attention**: Take *"Choose Your Neighbor"* invite flyers to the 20 closest homes to your listing. Invite neighbors to bring friends or family who have talked about wanting to live in the community. Have special pop-by style gifts ready for the ones who *"bring a friend."*

Remember: Every piece of promotion must include your branding so that whether someone sees a post, a flyer, or a sign, they instantly know it's your event — and *your* listing. *You have a thriving real estate business and it shows.*

♥ Hosting with Heart

When guests arrive, you want them to feel welcomed, comfortable, and free to explore. A few special enhancements can create moments they'll remember long after they leave.

- **Warm Greeting**: Greet each person personally, offer a quick tour highlight, and let them know you're available for questions.

- **Light Refreshments**: Freshly baked cookies, a charcuterie tray, a coffee bar, or even bottled water with your logo creates a friendly, memorable touch.

- **Information Station**: Have property flyers, neighborhood info sheets, and financing resources available. If possible, include a feature sheet that outlines recent upgrades and unique selling points.

- **Atmosphere**: Open blinds for natural light, play soft background music, and ensure the home smells fresh and inviting.

Hosting with heart means being present and welcoming — not just for the sake of selling the home, but for building relationships with everyone who walks through the door.

Following Up with Visitors

The real magic happens in the follow-up. Collect visitor information through a sign-in sheet or a digital form, and always get permission to stay in touch.

After the Event:

- **Same Day**: Send a quick *"thank you for visiting"* text or email, with a link to the home's online listing for easy reference.
- **Next Day**: Reach out to gauge interest, answer questions, and offer to schedule a private showing.
- **Ongoing**: Add potential buyers to your database and follow up with relevant new listings that match their needs and items-of-value emails and postcards.

A thoughtful follow up shows professionalism and keeps you top of mind, whether they buy this home or another one down the road.

Looping Sellers Into the Success

Your sellers will want to know how the open house went, so keep them in the loop with a friendly, detailed recap:

- How many visitors attended
- General feedback from attendees
- Any strong interest or second-showing requests
- Positive remarks about the home's features or presentation

When sellers see your positive energy, effort, and communication, they not only feel supported, they trust you even more.

This trust is what turns a good agent-client relationship into a great one.

🍸 Little Extras That Make a Big Impression

An open house is more than a home tour, it's a chance to create a mini event that buyers remember long after they leave. A few thoughtful touches can make your listing stand out in a sea of sameness.

A Home for All Seasons

Ask your seller for photos of the property during all times of the year. If it is winter, and your clients have pictures of summer flowers and backyard barbecues, ask if you can display some of these photos during the open house.

A Signature Treat or Drink

Instead of a generic snack table, offer something tied to the home's personality or the season. Hot apple cider and mini pumpkin muffins in the fall, lemonade with fresh mint in the summer, or cookies shaped like houses any time of year. **Bonus:** Print the recipe and send visitors home with it, complete with your branding.

Award-Winning Performance 🎖️

An open house is more than a couple of hours on a Sunday afternoon, it's a carefully planned event that showcases your expertise, your marketing skills, and your commitment to both buyers and sellers. When you plan with purpose, host with heart, and follow up with care, you turn a simple showing into a standout experience.

🔑 Key Reflections

How can I make each open house a true reflection of my professionalism and personality?

_____

_____

_____

_____

_____

What small touches could I add to make my open houses more memorable for visitors?

_____

_____

_____

_____

_____

How can I better communicate the results and impact of open houses with my sellers?

_____

_____

_____

_____

_____

_____

NOTES

DOODLES

CHAPTER 7

Under CONTRACT
What Happens Next?

> *Real success is built on real connection.*

From Offer to Agreement: The First Step to "Under Contract"

Before you can guide your sellers through the *"under contract"* stage, there's a pivotal moment: reviewing and accepting the offer. This is where your expertise, market insight, and negotiation skills shine.

When a buyer's agent presents an offer, it will typically arrive in writing, accompanied by the buyer's pre-approval or proof of funds. In multiple-offer situations, you may receive several at once, each with unique terms. Your role is to help your sellers understand not only the numbers, but the story behind each offer.

Key Points to Review Together:

- **Price** – How it compares to list price, recent sales, and market activity.
- **Financing** – Cash, conventional, FHA, VA; each comes with its own considerations and timelines.
- **Contingencies and Terms** – Inspection, appraisal, financing, need to sell a property, etc.
- **Closing Timeline** – Whether it matches your seller's ideal move-out date.
- **Inclusions/Exclusions** – Items the buyer wants included in the sale *(appliances, fixtures, furniture)*.
- **Earnest Money** – The size of the deposit and what it signals about buyer commitment.

Be sure to discuss each part of the offer and any addenda items. Allow the seller to ask questions and even vent when they feel the offer isn't reflecting their home's value. Your responsibility is negotiating with the seller as well as the buyer's agent. You will give them options and help them understand how each of those options may work for them.

If an offer is strong but not perfect, you may suggest a counteroffer to adjust terms while keeping the buyer engaged. Sometimes the highest price isn't the best choice. The best offer is often the one with the strongest combination of price, terms, and likelihood of closing smoothly.

Throughout the offer process, your sellers should feel supported, informed, and confident in their decision. This is a moment of both excitement and pressure, and your steady presence helps turn what could be overwhelming into a clear, guided choice that sets the stage for a successful closing.

👥 Clear Communication with Sellers: What Happens Now

Once the offer has been negotiated and accepted, your sellers may think the hardest part is over. But in reality, the work has only shifted into the next phase. Now, your job is to guide them through the series of steps that take them from "offer accepted" to *"keys handed over."*

Start by laying out the big picture:

- Key dates and deadlines from the contract.
- Upcoming inspections or appraisals.
- What to expect from the buyer's agent, lender, and title company.

Give them a simple **transaction timeline** that's easy to reference. This single visual can prevent confusion, minimize anxious calls, and set the tone for a smooth transaction.

Explaining Contingencies, Due Diligence, and Timelines 💬

One of the most valuable things you can do at this stage is translate *"real estate speak"* into everyday language that your sellers can understand. Calmly walk them through each contingency:

- **Earnest Money Deposit** - When it will be received and where it will go.
- **Inspection Period/Due Diligence** – When the inspections will take place, what types they might order, and how requests for repairs are typically handled.
- **Appraisal** – Why it's required, how it's scheduled, and what happens if it comes in low.
- **Financing** – The steps the buyer's lender must complete, and how this can impact the timeline.

When sellers understand each step in advance, they are less likely to panic if issues arise. This knowledge builds trust and positions you as their calm, capable guide.

📄 How to Present and Explain the Title Report

The **Title Report** is one of the least understood documents in the transaction. Yet it's one of the most important. Explain to your sellers that this report shows the property's legal ownership history and any encumbrances *(like liens, easements, or unpaid taxes)*.

Review the report together, pointing out anything that might need attention before closing. This not only protects your sellers from surprises but also demonstrates your attention to detail and commitment to a smooth transaction. Ask your title company for their *"Title Tips"* and give a copy of this valuable FAQs guide to your sellers to help them understand how to read their title report.

Your Custom Checklist, Items of Value, and Templates

Your sellers will appreciate having a clear checklist of what's expected of them and when. This might include:

- Scheduling movers
- Transferring utilities
- Final yard maintenance before closing
- Leaving behind appliance manuals and keys

Add extra value by sharing your branded *"Items of Value,"* such as:

- **How to Prepare for the Home Inspection**
- **Pre-Appraisal Checklist**
- **Moving Tips and Checklist**
- **Utilities Connections** - numbers and websites list
- **The Closing Process**

Refine Your Under Contract Seller System

Create and use an **under contract checklist or action plan** for sellers. As part of this plan, you can automate and send strategic emails throughout the under contract process to explain what is happening before each activity or deadline. Attach your items of value to further assist your clients in understanding the process.

When you provide regular connections and organized, helpful resources, you not only make their lives easier, you establish yourself as their real estate expert and guide for life. You will also create lasting goodwill that may lead to referrals long after the transaction ends.

🔑 Key Reflections

How can I make the offer review process less over-whelming and more empowering for my sellers?

_____

_____

_____

_____

What systems or visuals could I use to make the *"under contract"* stage crystal clear?

_____

_____

_____

_____

How can I turn my checklists and resources into tools that sellers will rave about *(and share with friends)*?

_____

_____

_____

_____

_____

_____

NOTES

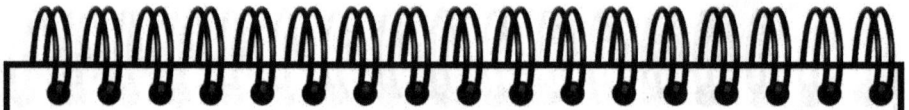

DOODLES

CHAPTER 8

CLOSING TIME
From Contract to Keys

⊗ Guiding Sellers with Confidence

A great agent guides every sale to a happy close.

Once the contract is signed and all parties are on board, the focus shifts to fulfilling the remaining terms so your sellers can hand over the keys with pride and peace of mind. While this stage may seem straightforward, it's often where emotions run highest. A skilled and caring agent knows how to keep the process on track while keeping everyone calm and focused.

This is the time to proactively lead, not just react. Your sellers should never wonder, *"What's next?"* They should hear it from you first, clearly and confidently. Learn to anticipate their questions and answer them before they even need to ask.

Navigating Inspections with Ease 📍

The **due diligence period** can be one of the most nerve-wracking parts of the transaction for sellers. Even well-maintained homes can produce a long list of findings from a buyer's home inspection. Here's where you can help your sellers stay grounded:

- **Prepare them in advance** by explaining that buyers often request repairs or credits, even for minor issues.
- **Review the inspection findings** and/or repairs addendum together, focusing on what's reasonable and what's negotiable.
- **Advise on response strategy**, whether that's agreeing to certain repairs, offering a credit, or standing firm. Your seller has options.

Your calm, fact-based approach helps sellers feel empowered rather than defensive.

🏠 Appraisal: Setting Expectations

The appraisal is another critical milestone.

- Explain the process, who orders it, and why it matters to the buyer's financing.
- Share that the appraiser's role is to determine market value based on comparable sales, not to favor one party.
- If the appraisal comes in low, walk through the options: renegotiate the price, have the buyer make up the difference, or challenge the appraisal with additional comparables.

By preparing sellers ahead of time, you prevent anxiety-based reactions and keep negotiations productive and moving smoothly forward.

Bringing It All Home 🏠

Sometimes, last-minute negotiations arise, from inspection findings to lender requirements. Remind your sellers that these adjustments aren't a sign that the deal is falling apart; they're often just part of fine tuning the path to closing.

Your role is to:

- Filter and frame requests so sellers see the full context.
- Offer solutions that meet the buyer's needs without compromising the seller's goals.
- Stay focused on the end goal; getting to the closing table on time and with terms that still work for your client.

📝 Coordinating Closing Activities

A seamless closing is built on clear scheduling and coordination. Create a simple, seller-friendly closing checklist that covers:

- **Final walkthrough prep** – home clean, personal items removed, keys ready.
- **Utility transfers** – when and how to schedule shut-off or transfers.

- **Document review** – making sure they understand what they'll sign at closing.
- **Moving timelines** – ensuring there's no overlap or last-minute rush.

Keep in close contact with the title company, lender, and buyer's agent so that everyone has what they need well before the closing date.

Keeping Sellers Calm and Prepared ☮

The last few days before closing can be emotional. Sellers may be juggling moving, saying goodbye to a home, and anticipating their next chapter. A few ways to help keep the stress at a minimum:

- **Confirm details early** so there are no surprises.
- **Reassure them** that minor bumps are normal and manageable.
- **Stay available,** even a quick check-in call can make all the difference.

The Closing Appointment

On closing day, most sellers will meet at the title company or sign documents remotely. Several days before the appointment, send them their closing details; date, time, location, what to bring.

Walk them through what to expect:

- How long the signing will take
- Which documents they'll see and be signing.

- When they'll receive their proceeds
- How and when to hand over the keys

A seller who knows exactly what's ahead will arrive at the closing table confident and ready.

🎉 Celebrate with Warmth and Professionalism

The close of a sale is worth celebrating! This is your moment to:

- **Congratulate them** on the successful sale
- Present a thoughtful **closing gift** (*optional but memorable*)
- Take a **quick photo** (*with permission*) to share their success story
- **Thank them for trusting you** — and remind them you're here for their future needs

The tone is important: heartfelt and personal, yet polished and professional. This is not the end of your relationship, it's a milestone in an ongoing connection.

🔑 Key Reflections

How can I better prepare sellers for inspections and appraisals so they feel in control?

_____

_____

_____

_____

_____

What systems can I use to make the closing process smoother and less stressful?

_____

_____

_____

_____

_____

How can I turn every closing into an opportunity for lasting client loyalty and referrals?

_____

_____

_____

_____

_____

_____

NOTES

DOODLES

CHAPTER 9

After the SALE
Turn Clients into LIFELONG Friends

Closing day is a celebration, but it's not the end of your relationship with your sellers. It's a new chapter. The days, weeks, and years after the sale are where you truly become more than a player in a transaction. You become a trusted, go-to person in their lives, the one they call for advice, referrals, or just to share exciting news.

Your sellers may have moved on physically, but emotionally, they still carry the memory of how you guided them. Staying connected after the sale reinforces your value, strengthens trust, and plants the seeds for referrals and repeat business. This chapter is about creating meaningful, genuine follow-up that keeps you top-of-mind without feeling transactional.

Show up with value... stay with ♡ heart.

📱 First-Week Follow-Up

The first week after closing is a golden opportunity to reaffirm your care and support. Your sellers may be in the whirlwind of moving, unpacking, and adjusting to their next chapter.

- **Check In Personally** – Call, text, or drop by *(if appropriate)* to see how they're doing. A simple, *"I was thinking of you today. How's the new place?"* goes a long way.
- **Offer Help** – Share the names of local service providers they might need; movers, landscapers, locksmiths, or home repair professionals.
- **Send a Handwritten Note** – Congratulate them again and acknowledge the journey you've shared. Handwritten notes feel rare and personal in today's digital world.

First-Month Follow-Up ✉️

After the dust settles, the first month is a great time to touch base again. Your goal is to remind them you're still here as a resource, not just during the sale but for all things home-related.

- *"How's It Going?"* **Call or Email** – Ask how they're settling in and if any unexpected issues have come up.
- **Small Gift or Treat** – Consider a coffee shop gift card, a welcome plant, or a basket of local goodies.

- **Helpful Home Tip** – Share a seasonal checklist or simple home maintenance reminders that align with the time of year.

🎂 One-Year Seller Connection Plan

To remain a trusted advisor long after closing, build a plan for touchpoints throughout the year. These connections should feel genuine and varied so your sellers look forward to hearing from you.

Ideas for Your Connection Plan:

- **Quarterly Calls or Emails** – Share a quick market update, offer a home tip, or just check in.
- **Holiday Cards or Seasonal Greetings** – A short, heartfelt message is enough to keep the connection alive.
- **Local Event Invitations** – Invite them to client appreciation events, neighborhood gatherings, or charity drives you're involved in.
- **Home Anniversary Love** – Celebrate their *"house-iversary"* with a card, call, or small gift. This is a wonderful way to mark the occasion and let them know you still care.

Gifts, Cards, and Seasonal Tips 🎁

Thoughtful gestures create memorable experiences that stick in your clients' minds. The secret is personalizing your touches whenever possible.

- **Gifts with Meaning** – Choose something that reflects their interests, family, or lifestyle. For example, if they love cooking, a quality kitchen tool paired with a favorite recipe.

- **Seasonal Tips** – Send reminders about winterizing, spring planting, summer maintenance, or fall home prep. Position yourself as their year-round home resource.

- **Cards that Feel Like You** – Instead of generic messages, write in your own voice. Your authenticity is what builds loyalty.

Becoming Their Lifelong Real Estate Advisor

Your ultimate goal is to be the first person your clients think of when they *(or anyone they know)* have a real estate need. This means:

- **Staying visible** without being pushy.
- **Offering consistent value** through your communications.
- **Being genuinely interested** in their lives beyond the sale.

When you've earned their trust for the long term, referrals will flow naturally, and repeat business becomes a joyful cycle. Your sellers won't just remember you as the person who sold their home, they'll remember you as the guide who made the experience seamless, supported them every step, and stayed in their corner long after the ink dried.

🔑 Key Reflections

What steps can I take in the first week after closing to make my sellers feel valued and remembered?

_____

_____

_____

_____

_____

How can I structure my one-year follow-up plan to be consistent yet personal?

_____

_____

_____

_____

Which seasonal tips or thoughtful touches best reflect my personality and brand?

_____

_____

_____

_____

_____

_____

NOTES

CHAPTER **10**

SIGNATURE Service
Create a Seller System with SOUL

> *Great systems create fabulous service.*

Your sellers deserve more than just a smooth sale, they deserve an experience so thoughtful, organized, and seamless that they can't help but rave about you to everyone they know. That doesn't happen by accident. It comes from building a system, your signature way of serving sellers, and infusing it with heart at every step.

When creating a soul-driven seller system, you're blending the best of both worlds: rock-solid processes that deliver consistent results, and a personal touch that makes every seller feel like they're your number one priority. You want each person you serve to believe you love them best!

Organizing Your Processes for Repeatable Success

The most successful real estate businesses are built on systems. When you have a process for working with sellers that you follow every time, you reduce stress, save time, and deliver a consistent, high-quality experience for every client.

Your system should cover the entire seller journey, from the moment they first contact you to well after closing day. Break it down into phases:

- **Initial Connection** – How you greet and qualify the lead, set the appointment, and send pre-listing materials.
- **Listing Prep** – Home walkthrough, staging recommendations, photography scheduling, and marketing plan confirmation.
- **Active Listing Phase** – Open houses, showings, weekly market updates, and feedback collection.
- **Under Contract** – Timeline management, inspection and appraisal coordination, and seller guidance.
- **Closing & Beyond** – Closing day experience, final thank-you touches, and long-term follow-up plan.

Think of it as your personal *"Seller Success Roadmap,"* a flow you can follow and repeat every time.

Templates, Checklists, and Your Personal Toolkit

Your toolkit is the heart of your system. This is where you keep the checklists, scripts, and templates that help you stay organized, professional, and prepared.

Consider including:

- **Listing Intake Form** – Capture every detail from square footage to special features.
  - **Prep for Photos Checklist** – Ensure every room shines on camera.
  - **Open House Supply List** – Never forget your signs, sign-in sheets, or fresh flowers.
- **Weekly Update Email Template** – Save time while keeping your sellers informed.
- **Closing Gift & Follow-Up Schedule** – Track how and when you connect post-sale.

When you store your templates in one place, whether that's a cloud folder, CRM, or binder, you can access what you need instantly and never reinvent the wheel.

Delegating and Automating with Care

Just because you can do it all doesn't mean you should. Delegating and automating are not about losing control; they're about creating more room for you to focus on what matters most, building relationships and guiding clients.

- Delegate tasks like photography booking, sign installation, or document collection to your assistant or transaction coordinator.

- Automate reminders, follow-up emails, and certain marketing posts through your CRM or scheduling tools.

The key is to **delegate and automate** in a way that still feels personal to your sellers. For example, an automated weekly update can still start with a warm, custom note before you add in market stats.

⭐ Consistency and Confidence Across Every Transaction

When your sellers know you have a *proven system,* and they experience it in action, their confidence in you soars. You become the calm steady guide they can trust no matter what comes up. And because you're delivering the **same high level of service every single time**, you build a reputation that produces more referrals and repeat business. Your clients can trust you to impress their friends and family as much as you impressed *them*.

As your business expands, your seller system will ensure that every transaction is handled with your same high standards. No matter how busy and successful you become, no person or task will ever fall through the cracks.

This system is not a rigid checklist. It's a living, breathing framework that adapts to each client's needs while keeping you grounded in your proven processes. Over time, you'll refine it and add new touches as it becomes **the signature experience your clients love**.

A great seller system doesn't just make your job easier, it turns every transaction into a story your clients are proud to tell. **And those stories are the seeds of your future business.**

🔑 Key Reflections

Which parts of my seller process feel consistent and smooth? Where could I add more structure or support?

_____

_____

_____

_____

How could templates, checklists, or tools free up more of my energy for connecting personally with my sellers?

_____

_____

_____

_____

What can I delegate or automate so I can focus on the parts of my business that bring me the most joy and value?

_____

_____

_____

_____

_____

NOTES

Listed to LOVED
The Heart of a Listing Agent

Selling a home is rarely just a business transaction. For your sellers, it's a chapter in their life story, one filled with memories, milestones, and meaning. As their listing agent, you have the privilege of helping them navigate that chapter with skill and mindful caring.

Confidence opens doors. Kindness keeps them open.

There is a unique joy in guiding someone from the very first conversation to the moment they hand over their keys. You've helped them prepare, market, and negotiate. You've listened when they were nervous, celebrated when they were hopeful, and stood steady when the path got bumpy. You've been their guide, their advocate, and their partner in one of life's most significant transitions.

The Lasting Legacy of Kindness and Competence 🤝

Long after the sign comes down, **the trust and warmth you built will remain**. Yes, they will recall your marketing expertise and negotiation skills, but what truly leaves a mark is your caring, patience, and ability to inspire confidence.

Competence gains you the contract. Kindness earns you a place in their story. Together, they **build a reputation that lasts** — one that travels from client to client, friend to friend, generation to generation.

🔥 Your Unique Energy is Your Greatest Advantage

There is no other agent exactly like you. Your way of communicating, your sense of humor, your attention to detail, your deep care, these are not "extras" in your business; **they are the heart of your value.**

When you bring your whole, authentic self into each seller relationship, you create an experience no one else can replicate. And **that's where the magic happens,** in the connection between professionalism and genuine humanity.

Your Call to Action: Serve with System and Soul

This book has given you tools, templates, and strategies to streamline your seller process. Now, it's time to make them your own.

- **Refine your system** so it's clear, consistent, and ready to deliver every time.
- **Embrace your value** so sellers feel the full benefit of having you on their side.
- **Serve with heart** so every seller walks away feeling cared for, respected, and understood.

Because at the end of the day, listings aren't just about getting a property sold. They're about turning a business relationship into something lasting and meaningful. When you work from a place of both excellence and empathy, your sellers don't just think of you as their listing agent, they think of you as their trusted guide for life.

List AND Last, My Friend!

You have the skills, the heart, and the drive to make every seller feel seen, supported, and celebrated. Trust your process, lead with kindness, and let your confidence shine. You're not just closing deals, you're creating lasting connections and leaving every client glad they chose you.

Now... go out there and turn every listing into a lasting relationship!

With Love,

Donna

NOTES

✨ MORE MAGIC ✨
Tools to Elevate Your Seller Experience

These resources are designed to help you put everything from this book into action with ease, clarity, and confidence. Use them, brand and personalize them, and keep them ready for every listing you take on.

BONUS: Your Head Start to a Smooth Sale Guide 🏠 SOLD

Create a branded guide *(or folder)* so your sellers can feel ready, confident, and organized before your appointment. It positions you as the expert right from the start.

Welcome & Introduction
Include a page with the following:

- **A short note introducing yourself** and expressing excitement about helping them sell.
- **A sentence or two explaining the purpose of the guide**: to help them prepare their home so your meeting is productive and stress-free.
- **Your contact info** and best way to reach you before the appointment.

What to Expect at Our Meeting
Add a paragraph or list of what you will discuss together:

- A quick overview of what will happen during your listing appointment *(tour of the home, discussion of goals, market review, pricing strategy, Q&A)*.
- A reassuring line about how you'll guide them through every step of the process.

Quick-Start Home Prep Checklist*

Give sellers a short, doable list to help their home shine:

- Declutter main areas and remove *excess* personal items.
- Wipe down counters, tables, and mirrors.
- Sweep/vacuum floors and tidy outdoor entry.
- Let in light. Open blinds/curtains.
- Mow lawn or sweep porch/walkway if needed.

(See full "Preparing Your Home for Success Checklist" on the next page)

Begin Gathering These Items

These will be needed to sell, so start gathering:

- List of recent repairs, upgrades, or special features.
- Mortgage payoff amount *(if applicable)*.
- HOA documents or fees *(if applicable)*.
- Utility info *(average monthly costs)*.
- Extra keys, garage remotes, security codes.

Questions to Consider

Encourage them to think about:

- Ideal timeline for selling/moving.
- Must-have terms *(e.g., rent-back period, specific closing date)*.
- Favorite features or stories about the home to highlight in marketing.

Helpful Extras

Add these to your guide:

- Seasonal tip sheet *(e.g., spring curb appeal checklist, winter cozy staging ideas)*.
- A *"pre-staging"* mini guide
- Your *"About Me"* one-pager with a few testimonials.

📋 BONUS: Preparing Your Home for Success Checklist

Declutter & Depersonalize
- Pack away personal photos and collections.
- Clear countertops and surfaces.

Deep Clean
- Floors, windows, baseboards, and fixtures.
- Freshen carpets and address any lingering odors.

Light & Bright
- Open blinds and curtains.
- Replace burnt-out bulbs with warm, neutral lighting.

Quick Fixes with Big Impact
- Touch up paint in high-traffic areas.
- Repair squeaky doors, loose handles, and leaky faucets.
- Refresh landscaping with trimmed shrubs, weeded beds, and seasonal flowers.

Staging Tips
- Arrange furniture to maximize space and flow.
- Use fresh flowers, cozy throws, and neutral décor.
- Keep entryways welcoming with a clean doormat and seasonal touch.

Photo Day Prep Checklist
- Hide trash cans, cords, and personal toiletries.
- Clear cars from the driveway.
- Set dining table with simple, inviting place settings.

Showing Appointments Success
- Keep lights on and blinds open.
- Set thermostat to a comfortable temperature.
- Take pets with you *(or secure them)* during showings.

BONUS: Your Personal "Signature Service" Toolkit 🧰

Your behind-the-scenes lists and items for delivering your unique, high-touch service every time.

Vendor & Service Provider Rolodex

Your trusted, go-to team who helps you get homes market-ready. Make a list of your service providers and their contact information.

- Photographer
- Videographer / 3D Tours
- House Cleaner
- Carpet Cleaner
- Painter
- Handyperson
- Landscaper
- Window Cleaner
- Junk Removal
- Stager

Your Signature Extras

Your personal touches that leave clients feeling cared for.

- Listing Launch Gift
- Under Contract Celebration
- Closing Day Gift
- Handwritten Notes
- Seasonal Touches *(flowers, holiday cards)*

Templates, Scripts & Checklists

So you can work smarter and stay on brand.

- Listing Prep Checklist
- Closing Week Countdown
- Showing Feedback Request Script
- Post-Closing Follow-Up Schedule
- Social Media Post Templates

How to Use This Toolkit

Update it regularly. Exchange vendors and services as your business evolves. Follow it consistently. Your clients will always experience the same polished, professional service, no matter how busy you are.

✉ BONUS: Weekly Market Update Sample

Once a week, send a market update to your sellers. This will keep communication lines open and also educate them about the current market and how to use best practices for selling their property. You can also include one of your items of value with each email.

Subject: Weekly Market Update and Pricing Your Home Right

Dear [Sellers' Names] -

When we listed your home, we ran a Comparable Market Analysis to help us determine the best selling price for your home. Please check out the attachment, *"Pricing Properties to Sell."* This tool outlines how a comparable analysis works, why pricing is so important in today's market, and what sellers can do to ensure that their home is priced strategically.

I have also attached new listings, new under contracts and new solds in your area for the market period. Please let me know if you have any questions about what's happened recently in the market.

Here are the links to online tours and advertising:

[Copy and paste virtual tour and site links here]

Marketing Period:
Sign Inquiries:
Number of Calls:
Number of Showings:
Showing Feedback:

Property Flyers: Please let me know if it looks like we are getting down to 10 or so flyers so I can send you some more!

Warmly,

[Signature Line or Banner]

🏠 BONUS: Surprise and Delight at Your Open House

Here are more fun, event-style open house ideas designed to feel warm, community-minded, and just a little unexpected, so guests leave with both a smile and your name top of mind:

The Neighborhood Connection Table
Create a space with maps, local menus, school info, points of interest, places to visit, and flyers for community events. Buyers often fall in love with more than just the house. They become attached to "the feels" of the lifestyle. Showing that you know and love the area reinforces your value as the go-to neighborhood expert. Even the family next door will appreciate what you are showing potential buyers at your open house and remember you when it's time for them to sell.

Interactive "Love This Home" Wall
Set up a small easel or bulletin board with colorful sticky notes where guests can jot down what they love most about the home. This will start people talking, create a positive buzz, and give you positive feedback to share with the seller.

Seasonal Mini-Events
Add a seasonal twist to your open house to make it memorable. Spring? Hand out mini potted herbs or flower seed packets. Summer? Offer a lemonade stand for kids *(and kids at heart)*. Winter? A cozy hot chocolate bar with marshmallows and whipped cream. Tiny takeaways go a long way in making the home and your event stand out.

"Imagine Your Life Here" Photo Corner

Set up a simple, staged vignette, maybe the front porch with a basket of flowers, or the kitchen island with coffee mugs, and **invite visitors to take a quick photo**. Use a small sign that says, *"Share your best smile, #HomeSweet [StreetName]."* It's playful, it's social media friendly, and it helps guests picture themselves living there.

Sweet & Savory Sampling Station

Partner with a local bakery, coffee shop, or specialty food store to feature small bites or sips. This not only adds to the hospitality factor but also builds connections with local businesses who may send you referrals in return. Allow the vendor to leave business cards on the table. It makes the event feel collaborative and community-focused. Be sure to **advertise on all of your social media channels** that your open house will be hosted by... [local vendor name] so be sure to stop by and try some of their deliciousness!"

BONUS: Closing Week Countdown

A Smooth, Stress-Free Finish to Your Sale

As the big day approaches, these final steps will help keep everything on track and stress levels low:

7 Days Before Closing

- Confirm closing date, time, and location with your agent and title/escrow company.
- Arrange for utility transfers (electric, gas, water, trash, internet) to end the day after closing.
- Notify USPS of your change of address *(and update subscriptions/bills)*.

5 Days Before Closing

- Schedule professional movers *(or line up helpers)* if not already done.
- Plan your deep clean. Either hire professionals or set aside time for a thorough once-over.
- Ensure all keys, garage remotes, gate cards, and appliance manuals are ready for the buyer.

3 Days Before Closing

- Review your final settlement statement with your agent to ensure all figures are correct.
- Double-check that repairs agreed to in the contract are completed and receipts ready.
- Remove any items that were not included in the sale *(play equipment, heirloom light fixtures, etc.)*.

1 Day Before Closing

- Complete your final cleaning and make the home *"show ready"* for the buyers' last walk-through.
- Leave a welcome note, spare paint cans, and any helpful neighborhood info if you wish to go the extra mile.

Closing Day

- Bring a valid photo ID *(or 2)* to the signing.
- Take one last sweep through the house to ensure nothing was left behind.
- Celebrate! You made it!

BONUS: Self-Care for Success: Little Rituals for Big Impact 🕯️

Building a thriving business takes energy, focus, and heart. And that all starts with *you*. When you're running on full, your creativity, patience, and problem-solving skills shine. Here are some simple, doable ways to recharge, refocus, and keep your spark alive.

The 10-Minute Reset — Between appointments or after a challenging call, take a short break. Step outside, stretch, breathe deeply, or sip a favorite tea. A mini pause can reset your mood and energy.

Joy Sparks — Keep a *"joy list"* handy *(favorite songs, funny videos, or inspiring quotes)*. When your energy dips, choose one and enjoy it guilt-free.

Sensory Soothers — Engage your senses to relax: light a scented candle, play soft music, or wrap up in a cozy blanket. Small sensory touches can help calm a busy mind.

Move It, Don't Lose It — Even short bursts of movement like a short walk or a 5-minute desk stretch can improve mood, boost circulation, and clear mental cobwebs.

Hydrate & Nourish — Keep a pretty water bottle nearby and snack on energizing foods like fruit, nuts, or veggie sticks. The better you fuel your body, the better your business brain works.

Digital Boundaries — Set times for checking emails and social media so you're not "on" 24/7. Give your mind time to wander and rest.

Celebrate Small Wins — End your week by writing down three things you're proud of, no matter how small. Recognizing progress fuels motivation for the next week.

NOTES

NOTES

NOTES

NOTES

NOTES

NOTES

NOTES

NOTES

NOTES

NOTES

ABOUT THE AUTHOR

Donna Wysinger began her real estate career over 25 years ago with a simple curiosity about flipping homes. What started as a personal interest quickly grew into helping friends and family buy and sell properties.

Though she hadn't planned on becoming a full-time Realtor, Donna soon realized that true success would only come by trusting herself and going all in. She immersed herself in the industry, learning every aspect of the business while working alongside top agents and on highly successful teams. Over the years she has worn many hats: listing specialist, buyer guide, transaction coordinator, admin support, new homes specialist, marketing designer and coordinator, new agents trainer, new assistants trainer, and more.

With her strong background in design and marketing, Donna also helped countless agents grow their businesses by creating resources and tools that helped them stand out. Eventually, she partnered with her sister to build a thriving real estate business of her own, using the very systems and strategies she had been developing and teaching. Together, they built not only sales, but lasting relationships within their community.

Today, after more than a quarter century in the industry, Donna has distilled her knowledge and experience into the **Be a Better Agent** community and her series of quick-read guidebooks. Her mission is simple: to help real estate professionals grow with confidence, connection, and ease.

MORE BOOKS in the Mini Mastery Series

If you enjoyed this guide, you'll love all of Donna's handbooks for real estate professionals. Each book is concise, practical, and designed to give you great resources you can use right away. Scan this QR code to explore all of her books on Amazon. *And she's still creating more!*

www.ingramcontent.com/pod-product-compliance
Lightning Source LLC
Chambersburg PA
CBHW071946100426
42736CB00042B/2246